HAPPY THOUGHT

The world is so full
of a number
of things,
I'm sure we should all
be as happy
as Kings.

A
CHILD'S GARDEN OF VERSES
DAYBOOK

Compiled by The Blue Lantern Studio

Chronicle Books • San Francisco

January

1

2

3

4

5

In winter I get up at night
And dress by yellow candlelight.
In summer, quite the other way,
I have to go to bed by day.

Bed in Summer

MY SHADOW—

6

7

8

9

Joey's birthday!

10

11

12

13

14

15

I have a little shadow that goes in and out with me,
And what can be the use of him is more than I can see.
He is very, very like me from the heels up to the head;
And I see him jump before me, when I jump into my bed.

My Shadow

JANUARY

16

17

18

19

20

21

22

Dad's & birthday !

23

24

Black are my steps on silver sod,
Thick blows my frosty breath abroad;
And tree and house, and hill and lake,
Are frosted like a wedding cake.

Wintertime

25

26

27

28

29

30

31

Blinking embers tell me true,
Where are those armies marching to,
And what the burning city is
That crumbles in your furnaces!

Armies in the Fire

JANUARY

February

1

2

3

4

5

6

7

8

9

10

11

My bed is like a little boat;
  Nurse helps me in when I embark;
She girds me in my sailor's coat
  And starts me in the dark.

My Bed is a Boat

FEBRUARY

When at home alone I sit
And am very tired of it,
I have just to shut my eyes
To go sailing through the skies—
The Little Land

13

14

15

16

17

18

19

FEBRUARY

What are you able to build with your blocks?
Castles and palaces, temples and docks.
Rain may keep raining, and others go roam,
But I can be happy and building at home.

Block City

FEBRUARY

20

21

22

23

24

25

26

27

28

29

March

1

2

3

4

5

6

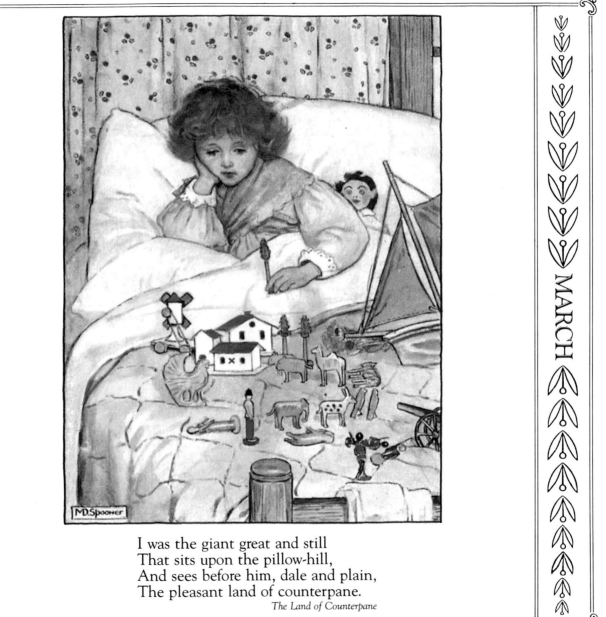

I was the giant great and still
That sits upon the pillow-hill,
And sees before him, dale and plain,
The pleasant land of counterpane.

The Land of Counterpane

MARCH

THE WIND.

7

8 .

9

10

11

12

13

14

15

O you that are so strong and cold,
O blower are you young or old?
Are you a beast of field and tree,
Or just a stronger child than me?

The Wind

MARCH

MARCH

16

17

18

19

20

21

22

23

24

I should like to rise and go
Where the golden apples grow—
Where below another sky
Parrot islands anchored lie . . .

Travel

25

26

27

28

29

30

31

MARCH

. . . slumber hold me tightly till I waken in the dawn,
And hear the thrushes singing in the lilacs round the lawn.

A Good Boy

April

1

2

3

4

5

6

7

8

9

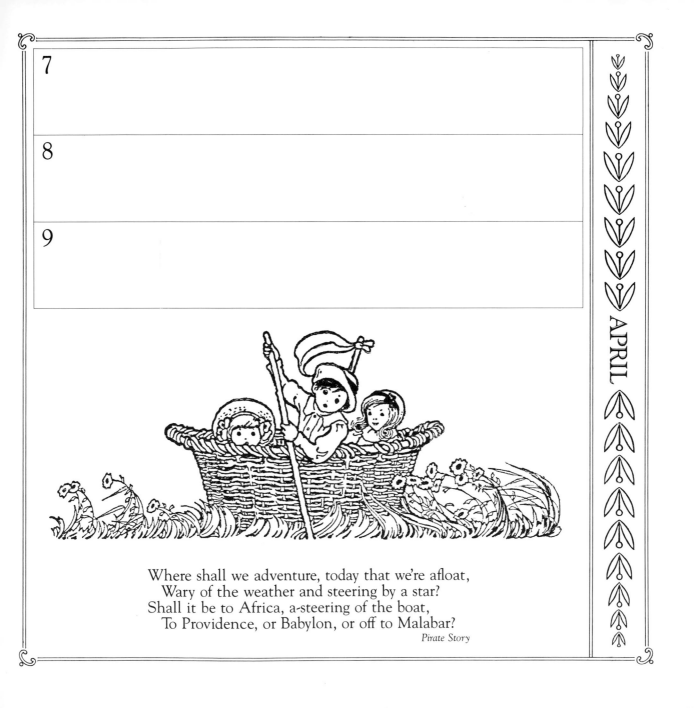

Where shall we adventure, today that we're afloat,
  Wary of the weather and steering by a star?
Shall it be to Africa, a-steering of the boat,
  To Providence, or Babylon, or off to Malabar?

Pirate Story

APRIL

10

11

12

13

14

15

16

17

18

Away down the river,
A hundred miles or more,
Other little children
Shall bring my boats ashore.
Where Go the Boats?

APRIL

19

20

21

22

23

24

25

26

27

28

29

30

Birds all the sunny day
Flutter and quarrel
Here in the arbor-like
Tent of the laurel.
Nest Eggs

May

1

2

3

4

5

A birdie with a yellow bill
Hopped upon the window sill,
Cocked his shining eye and said:
"Ain't you 'shamed, you sleepyhead!"
Time to Rise

MAY

6

7

8

9

10

My birthday!

11

12

13

14

15

16

17

How do you like to go up in a swing,
  Up in the air so blue?
Oh, I do think it the pleasantest thing
  Ever a child can do.

The Swing

MAY

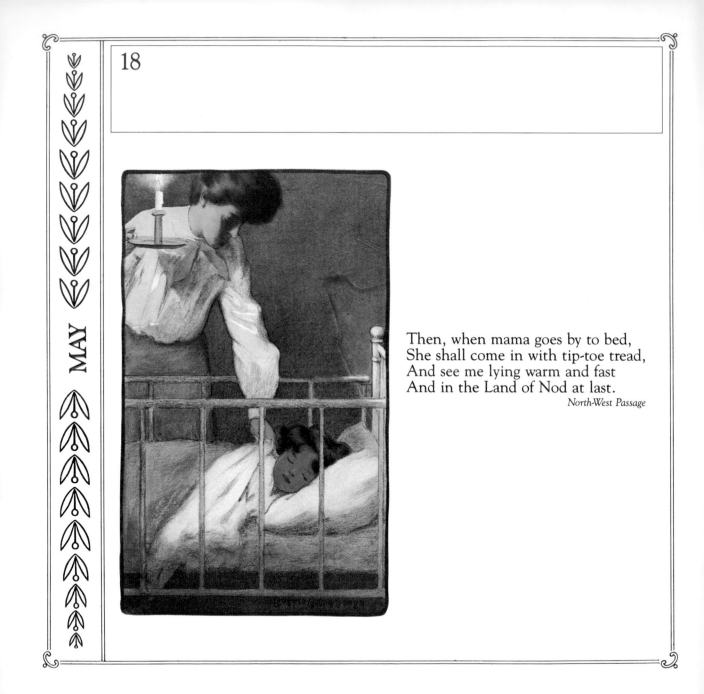

MAY

Then, when mama goes by to bed,
She shall come in with tip-toe tread,
And see me lying warm and fast
And in the Land of Nod at last.

North-West Passage

19

20

21

22

23

24

25

MAY

MAY

26

27

28

29

30

31

Sailing blossoms, silver fishes,
Paven pools as clear as air—
How a child wishes
To live down there!

Looking-Glass River

June

1

2

3

4

5

6

A child should always say what's true
And speak when he is spoken to,
And behave mannerly at table;
At least as far as he is able.

Whole Duty of Children

JUNE

7

8

9

10

11

12

Every night my prayers I say,
And get my dinner every day;
And every day that I've been good,
I get an orange after food.

System

13

14

15

16

17

18

JUNE

The moon has a face like the clock in the hall;
She shines on thieves on the garden wall . . .
And flowers and children close their eyes
Till up in the morning the sun shall arise.

The Moon

JUNE

19

20

21

22

23

24

25

26

27

28

29

30

JUNE

July

1

2

3

4

5

6

He digs the flowers, green, red and blue,
Nor wishes to be spoken to.
He digs the flowers and cuts the hay,
And never seems to want to play.

The Gardener

And when at eve I rise from tea,
Day dawns beyond the Atlantic Sea,
And all the children in the West
Are getting up and being dressed.

The Sun's Travels

JULY

7

8

9

10

11

12

13

14

15

Mom's birthday

16

17

18

19

20

21

22

23

24

When I was down beside the sea
A wooden spade they gave to me
to dig the sandy shore.

At the Seaside

25

26

27

JULY

28

29

30

31

O it's I that am the captain of a tidy little ship,
  Of a ship that goes a-sailing on the pond;
And my ship it keeps a-turning all around and all about;
But when I'm a little older, I shall find the secret out
  How to send my vessel sailing on beyond.

My Ship and I

JULY

August

1

2

3

4

5

6

7

8

9

10

11

The children sing in far Japan,
The children sing in Spain;
The organ with the organ man
Is singing in the rain.

Singing

AUGUST

12

13

14

15

16

17

Up into the cherry tree
Who should climb but little me?
I held the trunk with both my hands
And looked abroad to foreign lands.

Foreign Lands

AUGUST

18

19

20

21

22

23

The light from the parlor and kitchen shone out
Through the blinds and the windows and bars;
And high overhead and all moving about,
There were thousands of millions of stars.

Escape at Bedtime

24

25

H WILLEBEEK LE MAIR

26

27

28

29

30

31

Tiny woods below whose boughs
Shady fairies weave a house;
Tiny treetops, rose or thyme,
Where the braver fairies climb!
The Flowers

AUGUST

September

1

2

3

4

5

6

7

8

9

10

11

He has seen the starry hours
And the springing of the flowers;
And the fairy things that pass
In the forests of the grass.

The Dumb Soldier

SEPTEMBER

12

13

14

15

16

17

18

FAREWELL TO THE FARM

Crack the whip, and off we go;
The trees and houses smaller grow;
Last, round the woody turn we swing:
Good-bye, good-bye, to everything!

19

20

21

22

23

24

25

26

27

28

29

30

Out through the breach in the wall of the garden,
Down by the banks of the river, we go . . .

Keepsake Mill

October

1

2

3

4

5

6

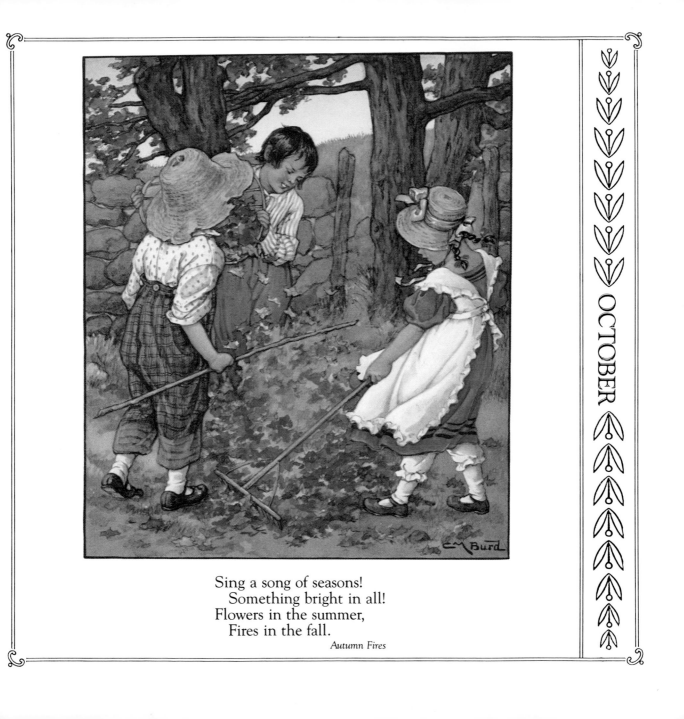

OCTOBER

Sing a song of seasons!
    Something bright in all!
Flowers in the summer,
    Fires in the fall.

Autumn Fires

7

8

9

10

11

12

13

O what a joy to clamber there,
　O what a place for play,
With the sweet, the dim, the dusty air,
　The happy hills of hay.

The Hayloft

OCTOBER

14

15

16

17

18

19

20

Bring the comb and play upon it!
  Marching, here we come!
Willie cocks his highland bonnet,
  Johnnie beats the drum.

Mary Jane commands the party,
  Peter leads the rear;
Feet in time, alert and hearty,
  Each a Grenadier!

Marching Song

From breakfast on all through the day
At home among my friends I stay;
But every night I go abroad
Afar into the land of Nod.

The Land of Nod

21

22

23

24

25

26

27

28

29

30

31

OCTOBER

November

1

2

3

Jack's birthday!

4

5

Whenever Auntie moves around,
Her dresses make a curious sound:
They trail behind her up the floor,
And trundle after through the door.

Auntie's Skirts

NOVEMBER

6

7

8

9

10

11

12

When the golden day is done,
Through the closing portal,
Child and garden, flower and sun,
Vanish all things mortal.

Night and Day

13

14

15

16

NOVEMBER

17

18

19

20

21

22

23

These are the hills, these are the woods,
These are my starry solitudes;
And there the river by whose brink
The roaring lions come to drink.

The Land of Storybooks

NOVEMBER

24

25

26

27

28

29

30

Summer fading, winter comes—
Frosty mornings, tingling thumbs,
Window robins, winter rooks,
And the picture storybooks.

Picture-Books in Winter

December

1

2

3

4

5

6

Whenever the moon and stars are set,
  Whenever the wind is high,
All night long in the dark and wet
  A man goes riding by.
Late in the night, when the fires are out
Why does he gallop and gallop about?

Windy Nights

7

8

9

10

11

12

13

14

15

The rain is raining all around
It falls on field and tree,
It rains on the umbrellas here,
And on the ships at sea.

Rain

16

17

18

19

20

21

22

DECEMBER

DECEMBER

23

24

25

26

27

28

29

30

31

Now Tom would be a driver and Maria go to sea,
And my papa's a banker and as rich as he can be;
But I, when I am stronger and can choose what I'm to do,
O Leerie, I'll go round at night and light the lamps with you!

The Lamplighter

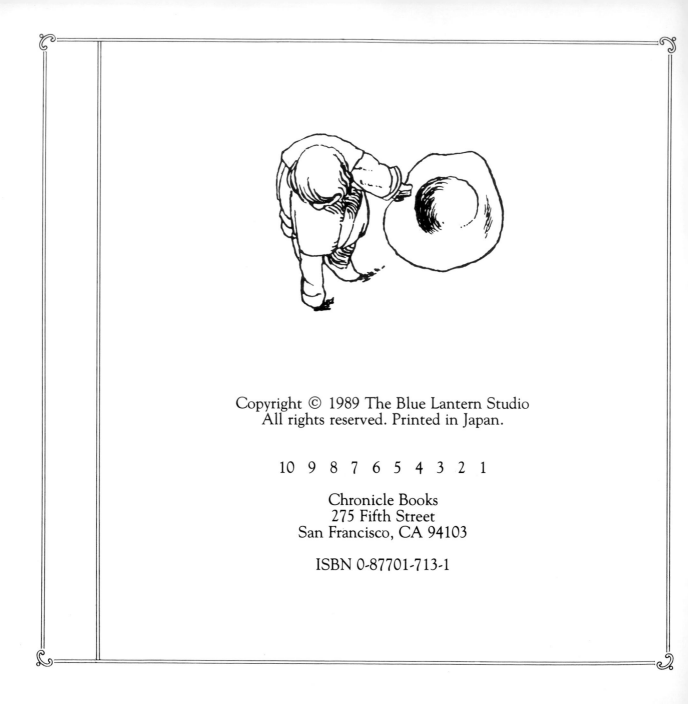

10 9 8 7 6 5 4 3 2 1

Chronicle Books
275 Fifth Street
San Francisco, CA 94103

ISBN 0-87701-713-1

ACKNOWLEDGEMENTS

ALL SOURCES ARE ILLUSTRATED EDITIONS
OF *A CHILD'S GARDEN OF VERSES.*
EXCEPT AS NOTED

Front cover	M. Dibdin Spooner, 1906	7/6	Bessie Collins Pease, 1905
Endpapers	E. Mars, 1900	(overleaf) 7/6	E. Mars, 1900
Frontispiece	Millicent Sowerby, 1908	7/27	H. Willebeek Le Mair, 1926
Title page	Margaret Tarrant, n.d.	7/31	Maria L. Kirk, 1919
1/5	Clara M. Burd, 1930	8/11	Jessie Willcox Smith, 1905
(overleaf) 1/5	Margaret Tarrant, n.d.	8/17	Jessie Willcox Smith, 1905
1/22	H. Willebeek Le Mair, 1926	8/25	H. Willebeek Le Mair, 1926
1/31	E. Mars, 1900	8/31	Jessie Willcox Smith, 1905
2/11	Eva Noć, 1926	9/11	Millicent Sowerby, 1908
2/12	Jessie Willcox Smith, 1905	9/18	Margaret Tarrant, n.d.
2/29	Millicent Sowerby, 1908	9/30	Millicent Sowerby, 1908
3/6	M. Dibdin Spooner, 1906	10/6	Clara M. Burd, 1930
(overleaf) 3/6	Margaret Tarrant, n.d.	10/13	Jessie Willcox Smith, 1905
3/24	Millicent Sowerby, 1908	10/20	E. Mars, 1900
3/31	George Reiter Brill, n.d.	(overleaf) 10/20	Millicent Sowerby, 1908
4/9	Millicent Sowerby, 1908	11/5	Millicent Sowerby, 1908
4/18	H. Willebeek Le Mair, 1926	11/12	Dorothy E. Russell, 1928
4/30	Bessie Collins Pease, 1905	11/23	Margaret Tarrant, *Verses for Children*, 1918
5/5	Millicent Sowerby, 1908		
5/17	Charles Robinson, 1896	11/30	Jessie Willcox Smith, 1905
5/18	Bessie Collins Pease, 1905	12/6	Dorothy E. Russell, 1928
5/31	Dorothy E. Russell, 1928	12/15	Bessie Collins Pease, 1905
6/6	Jessie Willcox Smith, 1905	12/31	H. Willebeek Le Mair, 1926
6/12	E. Mars, 1900	(overleaf) 12/31	Charles Robinson, 1896
6/18	Charles Robinson,1896		

A THOUGHT.

It is very nice to think
The world is full of meat and drink,
With little children
            saying grace
In every Christian
        kind of place.